Name

Date

This is where I'm headed.

This is the vehicle that will take me there.

This is the vehicle I wish I could take.

Bon

What or whom I am going to miss most while I'm away:

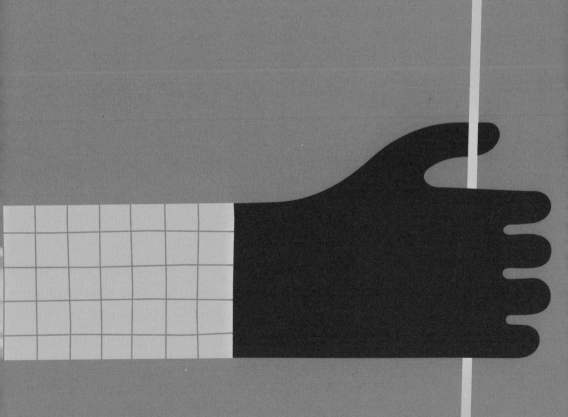

What I packed

This is how I feel just before I go on this adventure.

This is what I picture our destination will look like.

This is when we left home.

This is when we got to our destination.

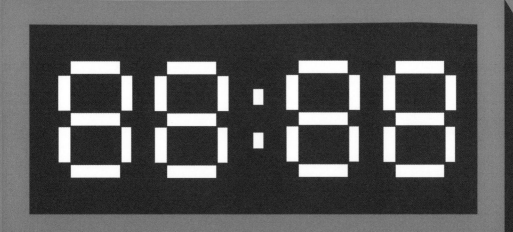

This is what time it was back home.

My fellow adventurers

...and some people I wish
were with me.

I'm staying in

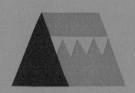

☐ a tent

☐ a house

☐ an igloo

☐ a chalet

☐ a camper

☐ a teepee

☐ a houseboat

☐ a tree house

☐ a hotel

☐ other

This is what it looks
like on the inside.

I researched this place and learned...

Isn't that interesting?

Audubon, Iowa, is home to Albert, the world's largest bull.

Alaska has a longer coastline than all of the other 49 U.S. states put together.

The World Championship Punkin Chunkin is in Bridgeville, Delaware. Some catapulted pumpkins fly more than 4,000 feet!

The grizzly bear is the official state animal of California. But no grizzly bears have been seen there since the 1920s.

Chicago is the birthplace of the first ever Ferris wheel.

In the Falkland Islands, sheep outnumber people 167 to 1.

Oops! I forgot to pack

(I wish I could magically ship this from home.)

This is what the perfect souvenir T-shirt would look like.

Ask a local

_____

Name

What's the best part about living here?

What's your favorite food?

Is there something we shouldn't miss?

Do you have a pet?

☐ yes   ☐ no

What is its name?

_____

Who is your
best friend?

_____

What's your
favorite
color?

Which do you prefer?

☐ sandals   ☐ sneakers

Something I would love to bring home, but it's too big

This is something new that I ate

...and it was

☐ incredible

☐ so-so

☐ surprising

☐ weird

☐ yawn

☐ hard to say

☐ so gross

☐ other: _____

Stop

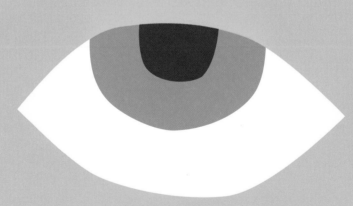

Look up.

What I see

Yes to adventure

Feels like fireworks and dancing

Smiles on the inside

MY
ADVENTURE
HAIKU

5 syllables

7 syllables

5 syllables

Today I spotted...

☐ a teapot

☐ a fabulous hat

☐ the number 3

☐ a large mustache

☐ something with green stripes

☐ a ball

☐ something upside down

☐ a feather

☐ a cloud shaped like an animal

☐ a butterfly

☐ a helicopter

☐ something blowing in the wind

☐ two red cars in a row

☐ an animal statue

☐ a small mustache

☐ a bicycle (extra point if it's a tandem)

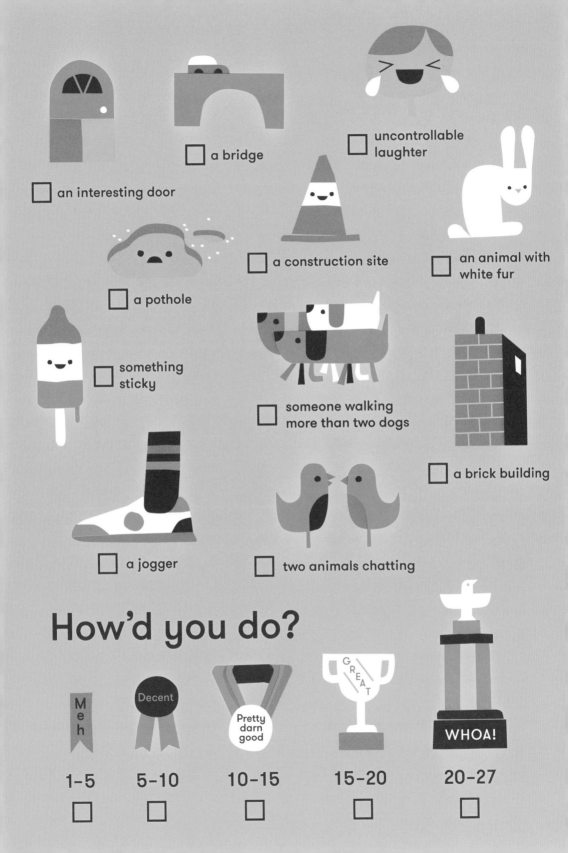

□ a bridge

□ uncontrollable laughter

□ an interesting door

□ a construction site

□ an animal with white fur

□ a pothole

□ something sticky

□ someone walking more than two dogs

□ a brick building

□ a jogger

□ two animals chatting

How'd you do?

Meh	Decent	Pretty darn good	GREAT	WHOA!
1-5	5-10	10-15	15-20	20-27
□	□	□	□	□

This is a map of where I am.

Key

railroad   water   street   forest   park   campsite   a funny thing   store   ice cream

skate park   airport   house   beach   mountain   hill   restaurant   I am here   totally unknown

Modes of transportation
I've used on this trip

other

If I could give this place a nickname it would be

Welcome to

This is the
local sports
team.

Today's adventure report

Today is:

Date:

I woke up at:

The weather was:

☐ ☐ ☐ ☐ ☐

What I ate:

Best thing I did:

Today's adventure report

Today is:

Date:

I woke up at:

The weather was:

☐   ☐   ☐   ☐   ☐

What I ate:

Best thing I did:

Something new I tried:

This made me laugh:

A special memory:

Overall, today was:

1	2	3	4	5
A day I'd rather forget	Let's not talk about it	OK	Way better than average	The Best. Day. EVER!

Today's adventure report

Today is:

Date:

I woke up at:

The weather was:

☐ ☐ ☐ ☐ ☐

What I ate:

Best thing I did:

Something
new I tried:

This made me laugh:

A special memory:

Overall,
today was:

1	2	3	4	5
A day I'd rather forget	Let's not talk about it	OK	Way better than average	The Best. Day. EVER!

Something new that I smelled

_____

It was lovely ☐ horrendous ☐ strong

Something really small that I noticed

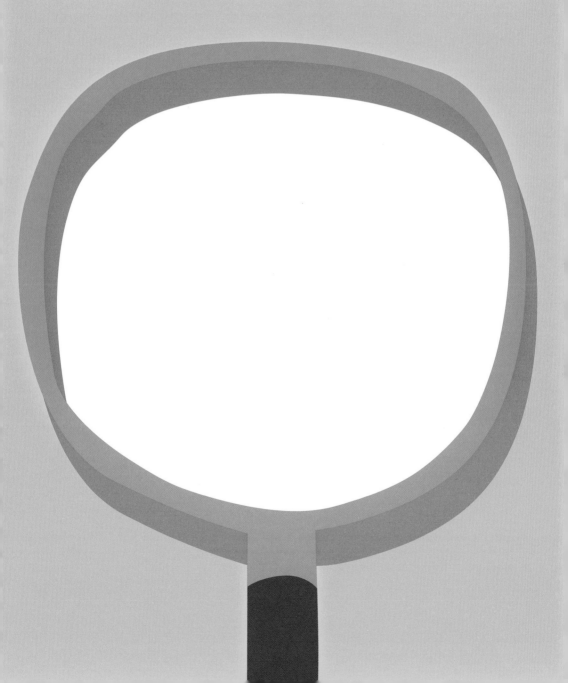

Something new that I saw

The waiting page

Sometimes travel involves waiting…
Grab a fellow adventurer and pass the time with some games.

white:

pink:

Total number
of things I can
spot that are

red:

blue:

green:

yellow:

This is how many people
I can see from where I am:

This is how many of
them are wearing hats:

Dots and Boxes

For two players. You go first! Join two adjacent dots
with either a horizontal or vertical line. Take turns.
When you complete the fourth side of a box, put your
initial inside it and draw another line. After the
grid is filled, the player with the most boxes wins!

Winner

Summit

Number of seconds
it took me to
reach the summit

Start

Another waiting page

Once upon a time,

Way out in

☐ the mountains ☐ the ocean ☐ the desert ☐ outer space

there was a

☐ yeti ☐ kid ☐ bandit ☐ snake

named _____ who liked _____

_____

_____.

Unfortunately, _____

_____

But fortunately, _____

_____

_____.

Isn't that

☐ unbelievable ☐ amazing ☐ just what you expected ☐ hilarious ☐ _____!?

The end.

My adventure
snow globe

An invention that would be useful on this adventure

Want to hear a joke?

What does a coyote
call its vacation?

A howwwwl-iday.

When I told it to

_____

I got a

☐ smile   ☐ chuckle   ☐ belly laugh

☐ weird look   ☐ head shake   other: _____

Color hunt

Search for things that are these colors.
Draw them in the swatch.

Really Red

Sunset Pink

Grass Stain Green

Taxi Yellow

High Sky Blue

Campfire Orange

Burnt Marshmallow
Brown

Deep End Blue

If I made
a movie about
this adventure,
it would
be called:

Something
I wish
I had taken
a picture of

I did some
shopping.
Check out
what I got:

Write, draw, and collect memories from your adventure.
Use the sticker shapes in the back of the journal to attach photos, tickets, or notes.

Write, draw, and collect memories from your adventure.
Use the sticker shapes in the back of the journal to attach photos, tickets, or notes.

Write, draw, and collect memories from your adventure.
Use the sticker shapes in the back of the journal to attach photos, tickets, or notes.

hi _____,

This is a drawing of me in front of

_____

_____

_____

_____ .

Wish you were here!

_____

hey _____,

This is a drawing of me looking at

the view of _____

_____

_____

_____ .

Huge hug!

_____

What makes a great adventure?

It's all of these things, and more! Earn each *Go!* adventure badge,
and stick it on the inside of your book jacket for safekeeping.

Meeting someone new

Trying a new food

Exploring somewhere
incredible

Seeing something
spectacular

Helping a stranger

Finding an unusual
souvenir

Walking what feels
like 10 miles

Going with
the flow

Doing something that
scares you a little

Sending a postcard

Making someone laugh

Learning the history
of a place

Completing *Go! My
Adventure Journal*

Planning the next
adventure

Design your
own badge

Design your
own badge

Find
everything
that flies.
Connect
them with
a line.

Adventure stickers to share

Wear one on your sleeve. Surprise a buddy. Give three to a stranger.
Wherever they land, these stickers are meant to make people feel good.

Nice socks!

Early riser

Brave meal choice

Fast walker

Really good hair

Stellar sense of direction

Contagious laugh

Thanks for helping.

Great smile

Hello sunshine!

Really silly

True explorer

BFF

A little cranky (but awesome)

Dance!

You're brave.

Super helpful

Have the best day.

Just lovely

Keep in touch!

Can you
spot these
hidden
items?
Helicopter
Hat
Herring
(that's a fish)
Hot dog

More adventure stickers

How many
canoeing
cats can
you count?

Stick stuff

Use these stickers to add ticket stubs, photos, lucky tree leaves, or any other relatively flat things from your adventure to your journal.

This is the next adventure
I'm dreaming about…